VOLUME 1 NUMBER 3

I0626495

PAPERBACK QUARTERLY

"A JOURNAL FOR PAPERBACK COLLECTORS"

CONTENTS

The Pecan Valley Press
Brownwood, Texas

The PAPERBACK QUARTERLY will feature articles and notes dealing with every type (mystery, science fiction, detective, western, adventure, etc.) and with every aspect of new, old, and rare paperbacks. Emphasis will be placed on the historical research of paperbacks, their authors, illustrators, publishers, and distributors; but the editors also invite contributions of bibliographical interest. In short, the only criterion for the editor's consideration is that the subject matter pertain only to paperbacks. In addition to articles and notes, the PQ will feature a section for the review of both old and new paperback originals.

The PQ will be published in March, June, September, and December of each year with a subscription rate of $6.00 per year or individual copies at $2.00 each. Institutional and library subscriptions are also $6.00 per year.

All correspondence, articles, notes, queries, book reviews or books for review, and subscriptions should be sent to 1710 Vincent, Brownwood, Texas 76801.

Billy C. Lee................Co-Editor
Charlotte Laughlin.........Co-Editor
Bill Crider................Contributing Editor
Martin E. Gottschalk.......Cover Printer
Pat Rawlings...............Text Printer

LETTERS

Dear Mr. Lee:

I have just received issue #2. Congratulations on getting off to such a good start. I particularly enjoyed reading about the Armed Services Editions, published by the Council of Books in Wartime. Only alluded to in Ms. Laughlin's article is the influence which many people believe these editions had on mass market paperback publishing. There is a strong school of thought present in most of the literature on 20th Century American book publishing crediting the ASE with setting the stage, if not creating a demand for good cheap domestic reading at the close of World War II. They demonstrated that a book market existed outside of traditional book-trade channels. Paperback publishers in existence both before the close of the war and those who came after, all tried in varying degrees to tap this market. They discovered that many in the market were pulp magazine readers. As a result, most publishers reprinted little beyond popular, category literature: mysteries, westerns, and romances. Exceptions were NAL and Pocket Books.

Several important people with backgrounds in paperback publishing were involved with the ASE. Richard Simon and Robert de Graff were directors of the Council on Books in Wartime and Philip Van Doren Stern (first Pocket Book editor) was general manager of the publishing program.

Another important person is John Jamison. He wrote a chapter on the ASE in his <u>Books for the Army</u>. He was at one time connected with the Editions through his work for the Library Branch of the Special Services Division. Jamison recently retired from the H.W. Wilson Publishing Co. Col. Ray Trautman, was the U.S. Army liaison with the Council and wrote and spoke extensively about the ASE. He recently retired as a professor of library science at Columbia University.

3

Besides Jamison's book, published in 1950,
two other books are useful to know about:
1. The History of the Council on Books in
   Wartime, 1942-1946. New York, Country
   Life Press, 1946.
2. Editions for the Armed Services, Inc.--
   A history together with the complete
   list of 1324 books published for American
   armed forces overseas. New York, Editions
   for the Armed Services, Inc., n.d.
Sincerely,
Thomas L. Bonn
Etna, New York

Dear Billy,
        I received PQ #2 yesterday and was pleased
with the issue as I did gain some more good
information. As it turnes out I was in the pro-
cess of compiling the same check list on "The
Green Door" issues and lacked a few authors and
titles, so I am indeed indebted to you as well
as to Howard Waterhouse and Rick Butler.
        On my annual book buying trips around the
country I have been able to locate Armed Services
Editions in most every city and State. Of course
the more popular titles are harder to come by as
numbers of serious collectors of specific authors
and titles continue to grow.
        Attrition---How many have survived? With
one third of the population moving each year,
think of all the books, magazines, & paperbacks
that get thrown out into the trash---millions?
I have seen numbers of them that were in junk
shops that had succumbed to the elements---water,
sun, dirt, etc and were just a short way from
being thrown into the trash for burial or to be
burned. Wherever I have been able to salvage
any of them--I have, even though there may be
pages missing.
        As to the millions that were sent over seas

4

(I read them on Guam, Eninetok, Ulitha, and other
south pacific atolls, during WWII) I bet that
95% of them were buried there.
    As to remainders? Warehoused? One day
somebody will no doubt uncover a small horde.
    Regards,
    M.C. Hill
    Bunker Books
    Spring Valley, California

Dear Mr. Lee:
I hope in time that your periodical narrows its
focus somewhat. To me, the term "paperbacks" en-
compasses a bit much: mystery, s-f, fantasy,
westerns, all of which are extensively covered in
journals of their own. I also worry about the
increasing tendency to academic over-writing in
the journal, something like what Armchair Detective
is now experiencing. Originally, I thought that
PQ would concern itself mostly with the history
of paperback publishing, yet I don't see that
concept emerging.

Anyway, a few comments on the last 2 issues: I
have a set of all the Dell mapbacks (in answer
to Query 3), and although I haven't checked
every one, your figures concerning the number
of pages seem correct. The article on Armed
Services Editions was nice, but I thought these
had been discussed quite a bit lately. By the way
the Library of Congress in Washington, D.C. has
a complete collection of these, donated by the
printer, Western Printing of Racine, Wisconsin,
who also donated complete sets of its Dell paperbacks and Big Little Books. Western Printing
produced most paperbacks from 1939 to 1976,
including Los Angeles Bantams, Pocket Books, Avons,
Dells, regular Bantams, Signets, etc. The Library
of Congress also has a copy of Western's card file,
which lists every paperback book (and digest-sized

book) they every printed--dozens of thousands.
I am now working with that file in connection
with a book about Dell, but I don't have the time
to work with the rest. Interested readers should
write to the Special Collections section or the
Rare Book Room at the Library of Congress.

Howard Waterhouse's Green Door checklist was
excellent, the best feature so far.

In answer to Query 9, I doubt if Pocket Books
will every answer your question. First, it
would take an enormous amount of work on their
part to check out such a question; second, they
probably don't even have the old records any
more. (Dell & Western did not keep their printing or contractural records--they tell me that
they shipped them to "some warehouse" some time
ago. Where no one seems to know.) Third, such
errors are common.
Best,
Bill Lyles
Silver Spring, MD

Dear Billy,
     Many thanks for PQ #2. Enjoyed the articles
very much, although Michael Smith should check
his facts more carefully. Almuric has had a
number of book editions: by Ace in 1964 and again
in 1968; by Don Grant in cloth in 1975; and by
Sphere Books in England last year.
     Thanks again, and keep up the good work!
Particularly liked the Armed Services Edition
article this issue.
          Best Regards
          Paul C. Allen
          Fantasy Newsletter
          Loveland, Colorado

6

Mr. Lee,
      Thanks for your kindness. Your publication
is unique, well edited and produced. Not the
least of its values is the one that awakens
dormant desires to start afresh.
            Jada Davis
            Dallas, Texas

Dear Mr. Crider,
      Congratulations on a job well done! PQ has
emerged as a worthy companion to TPCN in the
paperback collecting field. I only have two small
objections: your articles on paperback authors
tempt me to collect their works, which actually
wouldn't be so bad if I had any more shelf space
for another collection. The other objection is
that you don't publish the full address of people
who write the letters. I have fould this useful
in getting names to fill out my mailing list and
in getting correspondents with interests similar
to mine. If you adopted this practice I think
it would improve things by providing more lines
of communication between collectors. But anyway,
I am eagerly awaiting #3.
            Keep up the good work,
            Scott Owen
            Moraga, California

Dear friends:
      Belatedly I want to thank you for the copies
of the Paperback Quarterly and for the nice letter.
The interview came out just as I gave it, which
is not as common as you might think.
      No news here. Everything with me is still
about as it was when we visited. Ace Books will
reprint my old Ballantine book, Buffalo Wagons,
in November, and with it a new printing of The
Time It Never Rained, with new cover art.
      I have been told, though I don't know for
certain, that a student at some East Texas uni-

7

versity is doing a master's thesis, analyzing my
work. If I can become a college cult figure, I
may consider growing a beard.
    Thanks again.
    Sincerely,
    Elmer Kelton
    San Angelo, Texas

Dear Bill:
    Thanks for yours of the 3rd and for the copy
of Paperback Quarterly, which I found waiting
when I returned home from vacation yesterday.
I'm very impressed by PQ; it's a welcome publicat-
tion and I'll look forward to future issues.
Subscription check for $4 enclosed.
    Do you have any copies of the first issue
left? If so I'd like to buy one. Am particularly
interested in the interview with Harry Whittington,
for two reasons: first, because he has long been
one of my favorite ppbk writers; and second, because (coincidentally) I've just written an article
on him for an "encyclopedia" of mystery and detective writers which will be published here and in
England in late 1979. (The book will contain
essays on and bibliographies of the work of more
than 600 writers, past and present.)
    If you don't have any copies of the first
issue left, would it be possible for you to
photocopy the interview for me? I'd be glad
to pay for it, of course. Also, do you have
an address for Whittington? I'd like to drop
him a line in re the above-mentioned "encyclopedia".
    I'm afraid I don't have time to do anything
for PQ at the moment; but as soon as I finish
the novel I'm working on, I'll see what I can
come up with for you.
    Again, thanks for sending the copy of PQ.
    Best wishes
    Bill Pronzini
    San Francisco, California

Dear Mr. Lee:

We do have a complete set of the Armed
Services Editions collection of paperbacks and
it is my understanding that this is the only
complete collection in the country. Our collection
was a set that was discarded at the Library of
Congress and our very astute librarian at the time
was able to obtain the entire set. As to the
history of the collection I am not really certain
about the selection of the titles to be printed
in this form for our service men in WWII, but
I have been told that the titles were selected
by a committee of librarians for the American
Library Association. Our Asst. Dean for Public
Services has told me this about the collection.
He is in Chicago for the annual ALA meeting so I
could not consult with him before writing you.
He has expressed an interest in doing a study on
the history of the collection and its social
impact. He has not begun such a study, however.

Good luck with your new periodical.

Sincerely,

Joyce H. Lamont

W.S. Hoole Special Collections Library
University of Alabama

Dear Billy,

Received the two issues of PQ this morning
in the mail and I enjoyed them immensely. I'm
a paperback collector from way back and these are
right up my alley. Something like this should
have been done long ago. My only hope is that
you're not too under-butgeted and thus may not
be able to advertise and reach all the collectors
and institutions which would be interested in PQ.

I'm curious as to how many copies of each
issue are produced, what percentage go to libraries in Texas, how many go to libraries out of your
state, etc. I have a thousand questions. I'm

9

Dear Mr. Lee:

We do have a complete set of the Armed Services Editions collection of paperbacks and it is my understanding that this is the only complete collection in the country. Our collection in the country. Our collection was a set that was discarded at the Library of Congress and our very astute librarian at the time was able to obtain the entire set. As to the history of the collection I am not really certain about the selection of the titles to be printed in this form for our service men in WWII, but I have been told that the titles were selected by a committee of librarians for the American Library Association. Our Asst. Dean for Public Services has told me this about the collection. He is in Chicago for the annual ALA meeting so I could not consult with him before writing you. He has expressed an interest in doing a study on the history of the collection and its social impact. He has not begun such a study, however.

Good luck with your new periodical.
Sincerely,
Joyce H. Lamont
W.S. Hoole Special Collections Library
University of Alabama

Dear Billy,

Received the two issues of PQ this morning in the mail and I enjoyed them immensely. I'm a paperback collector from way back and these are right up my alley. Something like this should have been done long ago. My only hope is that you're not too under-budgeted and thus may not be able to advertise and reach all the collectors and institutions which would be interested in PQ.

I'm curious as to how many copies of each issue are produced, what percentage go to libraries in Texas, how many go to libraries out of your state, etc. I have a thousand questions. I'm

genuinely excited about your project and if I
get a little over-enthusiastic please bear with
me.

Would be nice to see more covers reproduced.
I really feel that this illustration of you 'zine
adds an incredible feeling of depth and is of
major interest to the collector (even if he has
the same pb in his collection; it's still nice
to see it reproduced).

This ties in with my second paragraph re-
garding your print run. If your per copy price
is too low to permit this extra expense for your
labor of love then I would suggest raising your
unit price to accomodate the extra cost, to say $2.

Something which may tie-in with your article
on Robert E. Howard is our edition of REH's major
poetry volume, Always Comes Evening.[See special
mention of ACE along with Robert E. Howard's
Library in this issue]

I'd very much like to meet and talk with you
about PQ. While I won't be able to make the
World Fantasy Con (Buddy Saunders, an old friend
from Arlington, Texas will be running a table
for me there) I will be in Phoenix for the World
SF Con over Labor Day. If you'll be there please
stop by my table and say hello.

 Best wishes,
 Chuck Miller
 Columbia, Pa

Gentle(wo)men,
Louis Black (Paperback Collector's Newsletter) sent
me issue 9 (May, 1978) in which is mentioned the
new journal: PAPERBACK QUARTERLY.
I like very much to subscribe to your journal.
To inform you of the paperback collector "scene"
in Holland the following might be of interest:
FURORE is a quarterly, edited and published in
Amsterdam by Piet Schreuders, a paperback collect-
or. During 1977 and 1978 articles in FURORE

appeared on the hard boiled school (Hammet, Cain,
etc.), the English Penguin, and paperbacks in
general. It seemed that a group of about 15 to
20 people in Holland were collecting paperbacks.
UTOPIA is a bimonthly that is published in
Rotterdam and of which I am one of the editors.
Each issue of UTOPIA is dedicated to one subject
(UTOPIA 7 on watertowers and solar energy,UTOPIA
8 on typewriters, UTOPIA 9 on television). We
decided to make a special issue on American
Paperback Cover Art that will be UTOPIA 10.
I went to the U.S.A. and visited all the "houses"
in New York. One of the results of this visit
was a conversation with Ray Walters who wrote
something in his column Paperback Talk in the
New York Times Book Review of December 11, 1977.
Since then contacts with collectors and cover
artists in the U.S.A. started to grow.
At the moment the situation in Holland is that
UTOPIA 10 is almost finished and promises to
be very informative with lots of illustrations in
black and white and in full color. Articles in
English by Mark Schaffer: A Glance at Paperback
History and Thomas L. Bonn: Interviews with
Norm Saunders, Robert Jonas, Lou Marchetti, and
James Avati. Articles in Dutch by Piet Schreuders,
Hans Mesman, Ed Schilders, Huib Opstal, and me
(all collectors). An interview with George T.
Delacorte, Mapbacks, Avati, Bantam, and Hollywood
of Paperback Industry. I will send you UTOPIA 10
as soon as it is published.
As a result of the interest in American Paperback
Art a group of collectors has formed to organize
the FIRST INTERNATIONAL EXHIBITION OF AMERICAN
PAPERBACK ART (APA) to be held either in Rotterdam
or in Amsterdam. APA at the moment consists of
five people: Piet Schreuders (FURORE), Bert
Haagsman, Hans Mesman, Ed Schilders, and Hans
Oldewarris (UTOPIA). Mailing address of APA or
FURORE is P.O. BOX 70053 in Amsterdam. Mailing
address of UTOPIA is Honingerdijk 245 in Rotterdam.

The exhibition will be next spring and at the
same time a very well documented catalogue will
be published. We try to make it a Dutch/American
coproduction so that there will be a catalogue
in Dutch and one in English.
You might not see it that way, but there is
a brighter side of American imperialism: we have
got plenty of Ace Double Novels and Dell Map Backs
over here in Europe.
I might contribute to your magazine with an
article called: EUROPE ON 25 ACE DOUBLE NOVEL
A DAY.
Hope to hear (and see) from you soon,
Hans Oldewarris
Rotterdam, The Netherlands

Dear Ms. Laughlin:
    Thank you for you for your letter and for
the copy of the Yellow Jacket, which I shall file
away among a horde of other such items. And, yes,
Tevis Clyde Smith did send me a copy of the first
issue of PQ, which I found most enjoyable. Of
course the article on the books from Howard's
library was of the most interest. I do have
the copy of Clark Ashton Smith's EBONY AND CRYSTAL
which was on the list; this I came across years
ago at Howard Payne and when I wrote to the library
about the possibility of my buying this when and
if it were removed from the library, it was sent
to me. It bears an inscription from Smith to
Howard; I had the pleasure of meeting Smith at
his Califoria home in 1959, only two years before
his death.
    I believe either you--or one of the other
writers (I don't have PQ to check on at this time)
stated that Karl Edward Wagner's Kane was a
continuation of a Howard character (Solomon Kane
I suspect was the character in mind). Not so;
Wagner's Kane is based heavily on the Biblical Cain.
    Yes, Mrs Shields[H.P.U. librarian] did send

me a xerox of the listing of Howard's library.
The only problem I have had is being able to
read the occasional listing due to poor quality
of original and/or xerox.

If ever I am back in Brownwood I shall take
you up on your offer to help in any research.
There is only one item that I know that requires
research: this is a copy of the Yellow Jacket,
and since I am typing this at work, I don't have
the date. But the date is given in the intro-
ductory part of the Bibliography in THE LAST CELT.
I seriously doubt that this particular issue will
ever turn up since I recall seeing a request for
a file copy for the library in an issue of the
Yellow Jacket less than a year later.

Best Wishes,
Glenn Lord
Pasadena, Texas

Dear Billy,

I have been asked by the editor of a book
to be published next year on book collecting to
contribute a chapter on paperback books. As I
envision it, the chapter would describe some of
the bibliographic and physical features of early
paperback books, outline some of the collections
which have been put together, and sources for
ordering and information. I am particularly
anxious to hear from people who are collecting
particular publishers, cover artists, subjects,
styles, etc. I would like to learn a little of
the difficulties you have encountered, but even
more of the joys that you have found in collecting
particular styles or types. Information on good
sources would also be appreciated. Thanks.

Sincerely,
Thomas L. Bonn
P.O. BOX 457
Etna, New York 13062

*(Tom's chapter is due Feb 1, 1979. Any reader
willing to help is encouraged to write Tom at the
above address.)*

EDITORIAL

As anyone who has ever tried putting out a magazine knows, it's not easy to get a cheap, full-color picture. Since the inception of PQ, we've wanted to have some color shots of paperback covers. After all, many collectors have their favorite artists. For this issue, color was even more necessary because we wanted to do justice to the work of Norman Saunders, with whom we had an interview planned. What we finally came up with was the color photograph that you may or may not have seen already. (We hope that yours didn't get lost in the mail.) We'd like to have your comments. Do you like this feature? We realize that the covers are very small. Still, the detail is quite good, and the colors are true. Expense will probably preclude the use of more than one color shot per issue, but if you like the idea, we'll continue.

Another point which should be mentioned is the dearth of submissions by writers outside Brownwood, Texas. We do have a new pb review column by George Kelley, a welcome addition, but we still need articles, notes, queries, or what-have-you. It doesn't seem right for all the knowledgeable readers of PQ to withhold their priceless information from our pages. We can get by, but we'd appreciate a little help from our friends.

Billy C. Lee
Charlotte Laughlin
Bill Crider

PAPERBACK WRITERS
-----BILL CRIDER

I've been informed by Billy C. Lee, the publisher of Paperback Quarterly, that a number of
letters which he's received have stated, or clearly implied, that many of our readers collect
paperback books mostly as objects, artifacts if
you please. In fact, he's that kind of collector
himself. I'm not. I started collecting paperbacks
because I liked to read them. I still collect by
individual authors, not by publishing houses. I'd
a hundred times rather complete my Harry Whittington collection that find a cache of mint-condition
Dell mapbacks (unless there were some Hammett mapbacks in the cache--I collect Hammett). Anyway,
what I'm saying is that I seldom buy a book that
I don't intend to read, sooner or later (usually
later). So as long as I continue to write this
column, I'll go on talking about the books and
writers I've particularly enjoyed.

That is, I'll usually talk about specific
books and writers. Not this time. This time,
I'd like to write a companion piece to my article
on "Paperback Originals" in PQ #1 and at the same
time respond to a letter by Dave Killian, printed
in issue #2. Mr. Killian asks that I make more
clear the reasons that the hardcover publishers
were so opposed to paperback originals. I knew
the answer (or thought I did), but I wanted a
respectably solid basis for my reply. I found
it in a long and excellent article in the October,
1951, issue of Writer's Digest, entitled "Gold
Medal Now Buying 7 Books a Month: $2,000 Minimun
Guarantee." This article puts the whole thing
rather bluntly: "Some of the old-time trade
publishers are really worried about Gold Medal
[the first really big publishers of 25¢ originals,
you'll recall], They feel that the newsstands
will put the bookstores out of business" (p. 16).
Why? Because so many $2.75 or $3.50 (those were

16

the days!) hardcover novels provided only an hour
or so of entertainment, and "at these figures,
entertainment was priced too high" (p. 15). Gold
Medal's 25¢ books were selling lots of copies to
lots of readers, and the hardcover houses were
afraid that they would be run out of business.
In addition, there was the "remarkable fact" that
Gold Medal guaranteed a $2,000 minimum royalty,
"based on copies printed, not copies sold" (p. 15),
an offer which in 1951 might prove attractive to
any writer, even one who had formerly written only
for the prestigious hardcover publishers.

The hardback houses defended themselves by
disparaging the quality of Gold Medal's books
saying that GM would have to rely on the "slush
mail" to provide new novelists and that Fawcett
wouldn't "hire the talent scouts and wet-nurses
to develop them" (p. 16). But GM had amazing
success. A total staff of about a dozen editors
checked around 300 manuscripts a month, generally
finding around 12 that contained "some promise."
These editors would work with authors "even if
as few as four chapters out of 12" showed some
merit, trying either to salvage the book (as a
rewrite) or to encourage the writer to try another
one (p. 16). The editors, many of them published
novelists themselves, were well-suited to the job.
They included William C. Lengel, editor-in-chief,
author of over 200 stories, two plays, six novels;
Richard Carroll, executive editor, playwright and
radio script writer; Webster Briggs, managing
editor; Richard Roberts, associate editor, author
of two novels; Karen Kehoe, associate editor and
novelist; and Barbara Hardy, head of the production
department (p. 16). Gold Medal "discoveries" at
about this time included Richard S. Prather,
Charles Williams, Gil Brewer, John D. MacDonald,
and Dan Cushman, names that should be familiar to
any collector of originals.

So what, asked the hardcover houses, and
added their final insult: "Gold Medal will turn

pulp" (p. 16). Well, as any fan of hard-boiled
fiction can tell you, "pulp" isn't necessarily
bad. In fact, to call Gold Medal books a direct
descendant of the pulps is both fairly accurate
and, to my mind at least, quite a compliment.
GM's own editorial requirements, whether consciously
or not, reflected the great old pulp values. The
editors told Writer's Digest they were looking for
1. An author with a story to tell
2. Smooth, fast-moving style of writing
3. Story content, consisting of a strong
   lead and establishment of a basic situation
4. Living, full-blooded characters, introduced
   and followed through believably. Minor
   characters should never clutter up the
   story
5. Wordage enough only to tell the story
   credibly and creditably (p. 19)
   Another accusation was that GM relied on sex
to sell books, and it's true that GM's covers
generally indicated that, as Writer's Digest tact-
fully put it, "the characters [in the novel] lead
a colorful sex life" (p. 15). Gold Medal preferred
to use the term "realism" in its description of
its books, though WD has these comments on some
of the best-selling titles: "The Tormented is a
study of nymphomania, Cocotte is the story of a
Paris street girl, and House of Flesh is what it
says" (p. 74). Most readers of such books are
well aware that the promise of sex is a lot
stronger that the delivery, however. Besides, a
lot of hardcover successes relied pretty heavily
on sex to sell books then (God's Little Acre,
Forever Amber) as well as now.
   There's a lot more material in the Writer's
Digest article than I have time to discuss here,
and it's well worth looking up if you're at all
interested in paperback original publication.
(Especially good is the reprint of a letter,
virtually intact, which GM's editors sent a
budding writer.) Next issue, I'll be back with
some writer whose works I like and collect.

DONALD A. WOLLHEIM

Donald A. Wollheim is well known to paperback collectors of all genre as an innovator in
the field of science fiction. I think it's fair
to say that his efforts in writing, editing, and
publishing have had a profound influence on pop-
ularizing science fiction since his Pocket Book
of Science Fiction in 1943. His editing career
began at Albing Publications Inc. in 1941. In
1942 he took an editing position with Ace Magazines where he remained until 1947. At this
time he became editor of Avon Books until 1952
when he joined A.A. Wyn at Ace Books until 1971.
In 1971 he founded DAW Books, Inc. and assumed
the additional responsibility as a co-publisher
along with New American Library. It has been
said that DAW Books, Inc. is "probably the smallest mass market house around." The average print
run in April of 1977 was 60-65,000 copies. Since
its beginning in 1971, DAW Books, Inc. has proven
itself successful, now issuing 5 new books monthly.
DAW books are aimed at a specific audience--S-F
fans and Mr Wollheim would be the first to admit
that S-F fans and collectors are very loyal.
Indeed, DAW Books, Inc. is only 7 years old and
their books are already collectable. DAW books
are designed to make them easier and more fun to
collect: First and formost, all DAW books have
a bright yellow spine making recognition very easy
for the collector. Secondly, the books are num-
bered consecutively. Thirdly, full credit is
given to the artist who designs the cover illustration and frontpiece(something paperback collectors have been pushing for a long time) and DAW
always has at least one illustration within the
book itself.

Unfortunately, Donald A. Wollheim has made
such an impression on the editing and publishing
fields of all genre (especially science fiction
and westerns) that many people are unaware that
he has written some first rate books himself.

19

A partial list of the books he has written or
edited are as follows*:

THE POCKET BOOK OF SCIENC FICTION,Pocket Book
     #214, 1943
PORTABLE NOVELS OF SCIENCE, Viking, 1945
AVON FANTASY READER, Avon, 1946-51
AVON BOOK OF NEW STORIES OF THE GREAT WILD WEST,
     Avon, 1949
THE GIRL WITH THE HUNGRY EYES AND OTHER STORIES,
     Avon, 1949
GIANT MYSTERY READER, Avon, 1950
FLIGHT INTO SPACE, Fell, 1950
AVON SCIENCE-FICTION READER, Avon, 1950-51
EVERY BOY'S BOOK OF S-F, Fell, 1951
LET'S GO NAKED, Pyramid #62 & 196, 1952
PRIZE SCIENCE FICTION, McBride, 1953
TALES OF OUTER SPACE, ACE D-73, 1954
ADVENTURES IN THE FAR FUTURE, Ace D-73, 1954
THE ULTIMATE INVADER AND OTHER S-F, Ace D-44, 1954
THE SECRET OF SATURN'S RINGS, 1954
ADVENTURES ON OTHER PLANETS, Ace S-133, D-490
TERROR IN THE MODERN VEIN, Hanover House, 1955
THE SECRET OF THE MARTIAN MOONS, 1955
THE END OF THE WORLD, Ace S-183, 1956
ONE AGAINST THE MOON, 1956
THE EARTH IN PERIL, Ace D-205, 1957
MEN ON THE MOON, Ace D-277, 1957
ACROSS TIME, Ace D-286,1957(psued. David Grinnell)
EDGE OF TIME, Ace D-362, 1958(psued. David
     Grinnell)
THE MACABRE READER, Ace D-353, 1959
THE HIDDEN PLANET, Ace D-354, 1959
THE SECRET OF THE NINTH PLANET, 1959
THE MARTIAN MISSLE, 1959(psued. David Grinnell)
MORE MACABRE, Ace D-508, 1961
MIKE MARS, ASTRONAUT, 1961
MIKE MARS FLIES THE X-15, 1961
MIKE MARS AT CAPE CANAVERAL, 1961
DESTINY'S ORBIT, 1961
MIKE MARS FLIES THE DYNA-SOAR, 1962

MIKE MARS, SOUTH POLE SPACEMAN, 1962
MORE ADVENTURES ON OTHER PLANETS, Ace, 1963
MIKE MARS AND THE MYSTERY SATELLITE, 1963
SWORDSMEN IN THE SKY, Ace, 1964
MIKE MARS AROUND THE MOON, 1964
WORLD'S BEST S-F: 1965, Ace 1965
WORLD'S BEST S-F: 1966, Ace 1966
WORLD'S BEST S-F: 1967, Ace 1967

many other "Best Of" for Ace and DAW.

*This partial list could not have been put together
without CONTEMPORY AUTHORS and M.R. Burgess's
CUMULATIVE PAPERBACK INDEX 1939-1959.

DAW sf BOOKS
No. 288 $1.95

THE 1978 ANNUAL WORLD'S BEST SF

Edited by
DONALD A. WOLLHEIM
and presenting the authentic
ten best of the year including
JOHN VARLEY
EDWARD BRYANT
JOE HALDEMAN
JOHN BRUNNER
HARLAN ELLISON
and others

PQ INTERVIEW WITH:

DONALD A. WOLLHEIM

PQ: Why did you decide to form your own publishing firm, doing only SF books?

DW: *In 1971, Ace Books was suffering from serious economic troubles due to some bad investments on the part of Charter Communications, who had purchased Ace after the death of its founder, A.A. Wyn. Because of this, it seemed to me to be a wise move to provide for my own future in the event that Charter went under (it didn't but came close). Having been an editor of paperbacks for over 25 years, it seemed high time to found my own imprint and do what I liked best·. science fiction. So I did, leaving Ace in October 1971, and founding DAW in November 1971.*

PQ: In the November, 1951 issue of Writer's Digest, Freeman Lewis, excutive vice-president of Pocket Books is quoted as saying that "'We have never felt that science fiction is a category with broad public interest, though we did issue The Pocket Book of Science Fiction some years ago. The figures from the field indicate that this has not been a satisfactory category in paper-bound book sales.'" (This is a highly ironic statement in view of today's market, of course.) Were you the editor of The Pocket Book of Science Fiction? What was its year of publication? Was it the first paper-bound SF book? Is it something of a collector's item today? When, in your opinion, did the market for softcover SF begin to boom?

DW: *The Pocket Book of Science Fiction, published
in 1943, was the first anthology of science
fiction, and the first book to carry the word
"science fiction" in its title. Since this
book went into at least five printings in its
first three years, it is hard to justify the
above comment. The market for softcover
SF began its boom with the titles being
published by Ace Books (under my direction)
and Ballantine Books (under Betty Ballantine)
regularly and monthly about 1953 and after.
These books were always profitable, if not
runaway conspicuous bestsellers, and helped
form the foundation stones of those imprints.*

PQ: As an editor for Ace Books, did you originate
the Ace Doubles? Where did you get the idea?

DW: *The Ace doubles were originated in conference
between A.A. Wyn and myself prior to the
launching of Ace Books. Books printed in
that fashion, back to back, with two covers,
had been done before, but as oddities and
never as a standard item.*

PQ: There is some controversy about the first
Ace Double SF book. Some think that D-13,
Cry Plague by Theodore Drachman, M.D., was
the first, though it seems more of a
mystery/thriller. What is your opinion?

DW: *D-13 was the first title to be technically
science fiction if you follow definitions
closely, but it was presented as a mystery
double. The first true Ace science fiction
was a bit later. I do not have an Ace index
at hand so cannot say exactly what that was
from memory, but it may have been a double
which included Van Vogt's The Universe Maker,
or a double with Leigh Brackett and Robert E.
Howard. [D-36, Leigh Brackett, The Sword of*

Rhiannon/ Robert E. Howord, <u>Conan the Con-
queror</u>]

PQ: In your career, your association with many
different major publishing houses has given
you a unique perspective of the paperback
industry. What do you see as the future for
the paperback industry? What do you thing
the future of SF paperbacks will be? Do you
think the SF market has reached its peak?
How do you compare the SF market in the U.S.
with the SF market in other countries?

DW: *I have not been a publishing grasshopper like
so many; I have been editor for only three
p.b. houses: Avon, Ace, and DAW. Paperbacks
are here to stay and it is the hardcover
fiction book which is ultimately to go the
way of the dinosaur. Science fiction paperbacks are also an established form and will
continue to be mainstay of SF now and in the
future--magazine defenders nothwithstanding.
I think that SF paperbacks at this moment
(mid-1978) have reached a peak and will re-
trench as meaningful returns come in during
the year to follow. The SF market in America
is stronger and larger than in any other
country in the world.*

PQ: How and when did you first get interested in
SF? In publishing?

DW: *I started reading SF as a boy in my teens,
with the earliest Amazing Stories, and have
been an addict ever since. I sold my first
short SF story in 1933 and have written
short stories and novels ever since. I
became an editor in 1941 and have been in
editing and publishing ever since. I have
been a publisher in my own name since 1971,
and doing very well, thank you.*

PQ: Who is your favorite SF writer? Why?

DW: *I would prefer not to answer this sort of question.*

PQ: Besides SF, what genre do you like best? Which non-SF writer do you like best? Why?

DW: *Other than science fiction, I have bought and edited just about every genre of popular literature. At one time I was the major buyer and publisher (for Ace) of Westerns in the U.S.A. I was an originator of the modern romantic-gothic novel. I still enjoy a good Western though I have little time for extracurricular reading. When I do extra reading, it is more likely to be non-fiction pop science.*

PQ: Does SF sell better in particular areas of the U.S.? What age group buys the most SF books?

DW: *In the past, SF seemed to do best in urban areas, and I believe this is still primarily the case. Best of all are college towns and places near Army posts. Which would indicate that the largest SF age group is between 18 and 24.*

PQ: Which DAW book has been the most successful as far as sales is concerned?

DW: *Hunters of Gor by John Norman, followed closely by the other Gor novels of John Norman, and by the works of Andre Norton.*

PQ: As of May 1978, how many DAW books have been published? About what percentage of these are paperback originals?

DW: As of May 1978, our collectors' sequence number was 291. Adding some unnumbered titles in our "Cap Kennedy" series, there were about 307 titles by then. About three-quarters of these were paperback originals.

INDEX OF PAPERBACK PUBLISHERS
IN PUBLISHERS' WEEKLY FOR 1950

Most people will agree that the best source
of information from the beginning of the paperback
era in 1939 to the present about paperback publishers is Publishers' Weekly. This is the first in a
series of an index of paperback publishers found
in Publishers' Weekly. Because of availability,
I have begun the index with the year 1950. In time,
I will pick up the 1940's. What follows is a list
of paperback publishers with the page numbers they
are mentioned on. The page number may contain a
mere mention or an entire article about that publisher. A "p" after the page number means that a
picture of that publisher's book is reproduced.
I have simplified the listings by grouping different
editions and trade marks of the same company under
one heading. For example Signet, Signet Giants,
Signet Double Volumes, etc have all been placed
under New American Library; Comet, Cardinal books,
Pocket Book Jrs, etc have been placed under the
heading Pocket Books. No effort has been made to
catalogue the publishers found in the "Weekly Record"
section of Publishers' Weekly other than to list
the page numbers of the "Weekly Record" sections.
The "WR" section does contain some valuable information about paperback books and publishers; especially dates of issue, size of books, price, psuedo-
nyms of authors, and often a one-liner about the
book.
This Index also contains a Monthly Title
index and a Quarterly Book Index giving title and
author. In addition, I have included the names
and pages of several exceptional articles and notes
concerning publishers rather than a mention of
one or two.
I hope you will find this index a useful
source of information for your particular paperback collecting interests. In indexing over 5000
pages, mistakes and omissions are very likely.

I would appreciate a card from anyone who finds
such errors.

Paul Hammonds
Washington DC

ARMED SERVICES EDITIONS:
v 159:   146
v 160:   566,568

AMERICAN NEWS COMPANY:
v.159:   1356

AVON:
v 159:   215,241,460,512p,518p,535,565,1356,1682,
         1892,2105,2328,2486
v 160:   130,546,863,864,1137,1139p,1341,1342,
         1824,2280

BANTAM BOOKS:
v 159:   150,214,222,223,241,460,518p,534,979,
         1002,1142,1682,1809,1947,1948,2104,
         2117,2537,2555
v 160:   130,546,570,571p,652,863,864,1137,1138,
         1139p,1342,1824,1976,2280

CORGI BOOKS(GREAT BRITAIN):
v 159:   1415

DELL:
v 159:   215,242,460,518p,519,525p,568,1743,2104,
         2117,2555
v 160:   130,653,863,864,1138,1139p,1342,1663,2056

GOLD MEDAL(FAWCETT):
v 159:   56,189,215 223,242,460,519p,577,1054
v 160:   197,566,863,864,865p,1138,1139p

LION BOOKS:
v 159:   215,243,519p,1427

MERCURY PUBLICATIONS:
v 159: 1743,2117,2650

NEW AMERICAN LIBRARY:
v 159: 60,215p,223,243,460,513p,519p,520,881p,
1356,1358,1743,1863,1864,1868,1869,1871,
1948,2104,2105,2118,2531p,2555
v 160: 214,546,547,566,569,570,572,653,703,704,
863,864,865p,1138,1139p,1342,1492,1493,
1663,1975,1976,2056,2123,2280,2382

PERMABOOKS: (at this time Permabooks was still
a subsidiary of Garden City Books. In 1954,
Permabooks was sold to Pocket Books, Inc.)
v 159: 243,519p,522,571,979,1071,1892,2078,
2078,2328
v 160: 214,570,864,1139,1140,1150,1179,1650,
1824,2124

PENGUIN:
v 159: 520,2105
v 160: 864,1139,1417,1647,1648

POCKET BOOKS:
v 159: 59,60p,139,146,150,215,222,223,243,248,
249,460,520p,583,584,979,1071,1142,1261,
1480,1573,1614,1728,1794,1809,1892,1947,
1949,2219,2328,2481
v 160: 32,214,546,566,639,703p,863,864,865p,
871,1130,1139p,1140,1417,1580,1646,2043,
2192

POPULAR LIBRARY:
v 159: 215,243,411p,461,520p,1002,1061,1809,
1948,1972,2105,2118,2650
v 160: 214,864,1139p,1140,1417,1824,1921,2056

PYRAMID:
v 159: 2219
v 160: 1580,1663,2056

THRIFT BOOKS(GREAT BRITAIN)
v 159: 1786

WESTERN PRINTER & LITHOGRAPHER:
v 159: 1880

WEEKLY RECORD:
v 159: 97-104;160-172;282-288;547-554;821-832;
        929-940;1004-1016;1072-1082;1184-1192;
        1289-1300;1369-1384;1439-1451;1502-1514;
        1617-1628;1683-1695;1744-1755;1810-1821;
        1920-1932;1982-1992;2119-2130;2253-2265;
        2358-2368;2429-2440;2498-2507;2556-2567;
        2651-2663
v 160: 70-80;131-140;215-224;376-385;514-520;
        581-588;654-664;714-725;815-824;891-900;
        1181-1189;1343-1356;1418-1428;1536-1548;
        1594-1607;1664-1676;1749-1764;1854-1868;
        1922-1936;1986-2003;2057-2074;2162-2172;
        2205-2215;2281-2292;2335-2344;2393-2401

MONTHLY TITLE INDEX:
v 159: 555-565;1083-1092;1514-1528;1822-1832;
        2265-2276;2664-2676
v 160: 386-394;725-732;1428-1439;1764-1776;
        2074-2088;2401-2412

DIRECTORY OF US PUBLISHERS ISSUING NEW BOOKS
DURING 1950:
v 159: 273-281

SPRING BOOK INDEX (Title & Author):
v 159: end of number 4

SUMMER BOOK INDEX (Title & Author):
v 159: 2131-2204

FALL BOOK INDEX (Title & Author):
v 160: 1190-1280

EXCEPTIONAL ARTICLES OR NOTES:

"Number of New Books Published Neared Total of Peak Year, 1940" v 159: 213-215.

"Publshers' Output in 1950" v 159: 241-244.

"Publishers Foresee a Good Spring Despite Shortages and Costs" v 159: 456-463.

"Spring Highspots in Paper Covers at 25 to 50 Cents" v 159: 518-520.

Anderson, Poul. *The Best of Poul Anderson*. Pocket Books, 1976.
The Peregrine. (Original title: *Starways*) Ace, 1956, 1978.
Question and Answer. (*Planet of No Return*) Ace, 1956, 1978.
The Man Who Counts. (*War of the Wingmen*) Ace, 1958, 1978.
The Night Face. (*Let the Spacemen Beware!*) Ace, 1963, 1978.
World Without Stars. Ace 1967. 1978.
Carr, Terry, ed. *The Best Science Fiction of the Year #7*. Ballantine, 1978.
Year's Finest Fantasy. Berkley, 1978.
Wollheim, Donald A., ed. *The 1978 Annual World's Best SF*. DAW, 1978.

Poul Anderson's fame in the science fiction ghetto is based on an astonishingly productive *thirty years* of writing. He's published close to fifty science fiction novels, over four hundred short stories, and still remains prolific.

Ace Books released new editions of Anderson's long out of print titles that were initially released as halves of the famous "Ace Doubles" series (it's amazing the way inflation ravages us; most of the Anderson titles were part of a double book which sold at that time for 35¢, now Ace asks us to pay $1.50 for *half* the book that sold for 35¢) with new titles.

The set of six books include brief introductions by Anderson, although they are superficial and not at all as interesting as Robert Silverberg's introductions to a similar set of Ace releases two years ago. Michael Whelan's covers dazzle the reader, especially the one that graces *The Man Who Counts*.

But, what of the individual books themselves?

Well, Anderson professes his work holds up over time. I disagree. On the whole, these six titles are fairly shoddy work and nowhere near the excellence shown in the Best of Poul Anderson.

Let's take The Peregrine first. Human civilization spreads through the stars like an overturned glass of brandy. As a by-product, a group of non-conformists, latter day gypsies calling themselves The Nomads, act as a trading link between far flung worlds. But, slowly, the Nomad starships begin to disapear...

The plot is interesting, but after a few chapters Anderson's characterizations break down and the reader knows what's coming.

Question and Answer has the same flaw. Earth is over populated and desperate for new worlds to colonize. Starships search for suitable planets. Finally, one is found. Troas. But the first Troas Expedition never returns. The second expedition is plagued by sabotage. When it finally reaches Troas, the second expedition finds... an alien race.

Question and Answer is a puzzle story, much like The Peregrine. But, when the characters give the secret away so early in the books, there isn't much to keep the reader engaged.

The Long Way Home shows more promise. It displays Anderson's love of byzantine politics with anyone involved in trading being a Good Guy. Earth is in a power struggle with the League of Alpha Centauri with the Society (interstellar traders) working both sides of the street.

In this situation Captain Edward Langely and his crew of the experimental starship *Explorer* suddenly become pawns of two empires. *The Explorer* returned to Earth with an alien, an alien with psychic powers, powers that could tip the balance to the side that possessed the alien. The alien escapes and the chase is on! It isn't artistic, but it's fun to read.

The Man Who Counts gained fame under the
title of War of the Wingmen, back when Ace
specialized in titles like Invasion of the Doom
Zombies. The book is famous because it's the
first full length appearance of Anderson's favorite character, Intergalactic Trader Nicholas van
Rijn, a mixture of Falstaff and Long John Silver.

The book is a survival epic. Van Rijn and
his crew crash on a planet where the food and
water is poison. They must make it back to the
sole human outpost before their food supply runs
out. One problem, however; the outpost is an
ocean away. Van Rijn needs the help of the winged
inhabitants, but they're involved in a bitter war.
There's a certain interest in how van Rijn cons
the barbarians, but it all seems so easy...too
easy to be believable.

The Night Face uses Anderson's favorite
device, the puzzle story, to explore a Utopia.
The Quetzal is sent to Gwydion to establish dip-
lomatic relations and negotiate trade agreements
with the newly discovered culture. The people
of Gwydion are strange; they have no concept of
war, theft, anger, murder, and the baser human
passions.

But three chapters into the book, the reader
should have the puzzle figured out. All that's
left is the melodramatic conclusion.

The problem with World Without Stars is that
it reads like a rewrite of The Man Who Counts,
without Nicholas van Rijn. In his place we have
Hugh Valland, who's lived a few thousand years.
The Meteor clashes on a planet between galaxies.
Hugh's task is to "organize a revolution by a
group of primitives against their telepathic
overlords; build with the help of those same
primitives a spaceship virtually from scratch;
contact, via that spaceship, a third group of
aliens and enlist their aid in returning home
across the galactic abyss." It's all a bit much.
And the ending is particularly maudlin.

I admire much of Poul Anderson's work, but most of Ace's rereleases are minor Anderson at best.

The best of Poul Anderson's short work is collected in The Best of Poul Anderson. "Sam Hall" is here, along with "Kyrie" and "The Longest Voyage." Also included is Anderson's best puzzle story, starring Nicholas van Rijn, "Hiding Place." The Best of Poul Anderson is an excellent collection, well worth reading and collecting.

The stories in The Best of Poul Anderson illustrate in the short form what Anderson expresses in his SF novels: the themes of struggle and collapse of civilizations, the distrust of governments, the importance of trade, the supremacy of outstanding individuals, and a faith in technology to solve problems. There are traces of racism, sexism, and sadism in Anderson's works, especially in the early works. Sandra Miesel, whose "critical" articles are found in a couple of Anderson's books, never addresses these flaws in her essays, preferring instead to deal with "myth motifs and dramatic language."

Poul Anderson writes of a cruel universe where individuals might beat the odds, but governments are always losers. Maybe Anderson's the Milton Friedman of science fiction?

Every year SF has its parade of "Best of..." anthologies.

The best of these is Terry Carr's Best Science Fiction of The Year series. The seventh volume includes stories by Michael Bishop, Lee Killough, Fritz Leiber, Bruce McAllister, Vonda N. McIntyre, Sprider & Heanne Robinson, Raccoona Sheldon, Lisa Tuttle, John Varley, and Charlie Brown's "The Science Fiction Year" wrap up.

Of these stories, Raccoona Sheldon (James Tiptree, Jr.) has the most memorable, a chilling tale called "The Screwfly Solution." It's stunning.

John Varley, who can do no wrong, delights

with "Lollipop and the Tar Baby." And I especially
liked Bruce McAllister's bittersweet "Victor."

Donald A. Wollheim's The 1978 Annual World's
Best SF includes John Varley, Joe Haldeman, Michael
Bishop, Edward Bryant, John Brunner, Harlan
Ellison, Raccoona Sheldon, Joan D. Vinge, James
E. Gunn, and Clifford Simak. The overlap between
the Carr and Wollheim collections are the Sheldon
story and Michael Bishop's "House of the Compassion-
ate Sharers."

I was particularly fond of Joan D. Vinge's
"Eyes of Amber" and Harlan Ellison's "Jeffty is
Five." The only story I found not worthy of the
"Best" distinction was John Brunner's "The Taste
of the Dish and the Savor of the Day." It's slow,
plodding, and not very interesting.

Finally, Terry Carr launches a new anthology,
Year's Finest Fantasy. Unfortunately, it's not
of the quality of his science fiction collection.
There are stories by Harlan Ellison, Woody Allen,
Avram Davidson, Stephen King, Jack Vance, Robert
Aickman, Julian Reid, Raylyn Moore, Steven Utley
& Howard Waldrop, and T. Coraghessan Boyle.

Clearly, the best stories are Woody Allen's
"The Kugelmass Episode" and Stephen King's brutal
"Cat from Hell." From there the quality drops
off sharply. Also, this Carr collection lacks
the "Recommended Reading" feature and a yearly
summation his SF collectiong collection contains.
I hope they'll be included in the next volume.

PQ INTERVIEW WITH:

NORMAN SAUNDERS

PQ: How did you first get involved in doing paperback cover paintings?

NS: *Originally I started painting pulp covers for Dell, Street & Smith, Fiction House, A. Wynn, and Martin Goodman---and when some of these publishers went into paperbacks, they purchased my paintings.*

PQ: The cover plays a major role in how well a paperback sells. If the cover is so important, why is it in your opinion that the paperback cover artist is often given no credit line for his work?

NS: *Most artists signed their covers at first, then some publishers gave a credit line or blurb----eventually the production of a cover became a big project with typographers and every one and his office boy----it.is no longer a personal project.*

PQ: How do you get your ideas for your cover paintings? Are you told what type of cover is wanted or do you have a free hand in making your own decisions?

NS: *Various publishers did it differently; some gave you a shooting script, some gave you the manuscript, and some just discussed the idea they had in mind----with different results.*

PQ: Do you read the books before you paint their covers?

NS: *Sometimes--or at least the section that pertains to the cover.*

PQ: What type of covers do you like to paint best? Of all the covers you have painted, which is your favorite? Why?

NS: *This is hard to answer--I believe dective and western--I really don't have any favorite--I enjoyed painting them all.*

PQ: Are you still painting paperback covers?

NS: *No--I am 71 years old and I prefer painting pictures for my own pleasure. I have painted pulp and paperback covers for 50 years. It's a lot more fun to paint to suit myself.*

I believe my first paperback cover was for Street & Smith--a paperback size magazine called "Pocket Detective" for 15¢. I think it came out in the September 1939 issue.

I painted both covers on Wynn's Ace double books Too Hot For Hell and The Grinning Gismo which was their first paperback.

I really have no idea how many I have painted--I'm sure it was my share.

[The list that follows was supplied by Norman Saunders and supplimented by Tom Bonn of Cortland, New York. Mr. Bonn informed Mr. Saunders that his Too Hot For Hell cover appeared in the March 1978 issue of PQ and as a result prompted this interview. Mr. Saunders says that this list includes probably less than 50% of the covers he has painted. Any collector finding Mr. Saunders' covers not included in this list are ask to send the name of the book to the editors of PQ.]

A 1950's photograph of Norman Saunders with
5 cover illustrations from the 1950's

A PARTIAL LIST OF PAPERBACK COVERS
PAINTED BY

NORMAN SAUNDERS

ACE BOOKS:
D-1   The Grinning Gismo by Samuel W. Taylor
D-1   To Hot For Hell by Keith Vining
D-5   The Scarlet Spade by Eaton K. Goldwaite
D-5   Drawn to Evil by Harry Whittington
D-16 Germinie by Jules & Edmond de Goncourt
D-17 Shakedown by Roney Scott
D-18
D-25 The Code of the Woosters by P.G. Wodehouse
D-26 Love in a Junk
D-26 The Impotent General by Charles Pettit
D-27 The Fingered Man by Bruno Fischer
D-33 Murder by the Pack by Carl G. Hodges
D-34 Feud in Piney Flats by Ken Murray
D-39 Quantrell's Raiders by Frank Gruber

READERS CHOICE LIBRARY:
4   The Powder Burner
9   Smoky Joe

LION BOOKS:
17 Dust on the Trail by Bennett Foster

BANTAM BOOKS:
206 Deputy Marshal by Charles N. Heckelmann
207 Short Grass by Thomas W. Blackburn
209 Hard Money by Luke Short
255 Badlands by Bennett Foster
261 The Wild Bunch by Ernest Haycox
726 Desert Law by Clarence Budingtpn Kelland
731 Sheriff's Revenge by Peter Field
740 Bullet Breed by Leslie Ernenwein
254 The Border Bandit by Evan Evans
715 My Greatest Day in Football by Murray Goodman
                & Leonard Lewin
799 Thunder on the Buckhorn by Frank O'Rourke

BALLANTINE BOOKS:
4   Saddle by Starlight by Luke Short
7   Blood on the Land by Frank Bonham
10 Concannon by Frank O'Rourke

POPULAR LIBRARY:
590 Gold Town Gunman by Ray Townsend

HANDI BOOKS:
134 Murder is Dangerous by Saul Levinson
135 Typed for a Corpse by Alan Pruitt
136 Dark Canyon by Tex Holt

BEST DETECTIVE SELECTION:
4   The Bloody Wig Murders
5   The Pool of Death

A CRIME NOVEL SELECTION:
1   Strangers Holiday

STREET & SMITH:
Pocket Detective----2 or 3 covers unnumbered

THE MYSTERIOUS TRAVLERS MAGAZINE:
This was a trifle over pocket book size. I
painted a half a dozen or so--

PHAMTOM BOOKS:
early sex type pocket books; I painted a half
dozen titles like---Sex-a-go-go and Tonight, She's
Yours, etc.

[The above list could not have been compiled without the aid of M.R. Burgess's Cumulative Paperback
Index 1939-1959 which is available from Gale
Research Company, Book Tower, Detroit, Michigan
48226]

ROBERT E. HOWARD'S LIBRARY
A CHECKLIST

The spring issue of PAPERBACK QUARTERLY reported that of the 268 books believed to have composed the Robert E. Howard Memorial Collection of Howard Payne College's Walker Memorial Library, 45 remain with the bookplate in place. Since then, two more books with the Robert E. Howard bookplate have been found on the shelves of the library. One of these books is <u>Black Bartlemy's Treasure</u> by Jeffery Farnol. A penciled note on the title-page of <u>Martin Conisby's Vengeance</u> (described in PQ #1, page 29) gives the following information: "Read 'Black Bartlemy's Treasure' first. This is a sequel to it." The second book found to contain the bookplate is <u>King of the Black Isles</u>, a book of poems by J.U. Nicolson. A third book, <u>Cimarron</u> by Edna Ferber, does not have the bookplate, but accession records indicate that it probably is the copy which was originally in Robert E. Howard's library. A section on page 35 of that book has been underlined twice, once in pencil, and once in ink. If we could be sure that this passage had been so emphasized by Howard, we might better understand Howard's unusual dependence on his mother. The passage reads, "Twenty-one, and the yoke of her mother's dominance was beginning to gall her. Now, at her own inner rage and sickening disappointment, all the iron in her fused and hardened."

Following is the third of four parts, listing the books in Robert E. Howard's personal library which were given to Howard Payne College in 1936.

England, George	Flying Legion
Erskine, John	Galahad
Farnol, Jeffery	The Broad Highway
Farnol, Jeffery	Guyfford of Weaves
Farnol, Jeffery	Sir John D ing[?]
Flagellant	Curiosa of Flagellants
Flagellant	Experiences of Flagellation
Flannagan, Roy C.	The Whipping
Fleisher, Nat	Jack Dempsey
Fort, Charles	Lo
France, Hector	Musk, Hashish, And Blood
Gilbert, William S.	Best Known Works of W.S. Gilbert
Gillespie, James E.	A History of Europe
Gold, Grace	How to be Happy
Gregory, Jackson	Six Feet Four
Grenard	Baker[?]
Grey, Zane	The Border Legion
Grey, Zane	To The Last Man
Gross, Milt	Don't Ask!!
Guenhen, H.A.[?]	Myths of Greece and Rome
Haggard, Rider	Allan Quatermain
Haggard, Rider	Ancient Allan
Haggard, Rider	People of the Mist
Hamlin, C.H.	War Myth on U.S. History
Hanshew, M and T	Riddle of Frozen Flame
Hanshew, M and T	Riddle of Mysterous Light
Harper and Newhern	Odd Texas
Harvard Classics	Poems and Songs of Robert Burns
Hawksworth	A Year in Wonderland of Trees
Hayes	Pol. & Cultural History of Modern Europe
Hemyng[?],Bracebridge	Jack Harkanay in Cuba
Henty, G. A.	Bravest of the Brave
Holmes, Fred	Indian Frontier Fighters
Holmes, Oliver W.	Autocrat of the Breakfast Table (2 copies)
Ingraham, J.H.	Throne of David
Inman	Wulmoth the Wanderer
Jennson	Natural History of Animals

Johnson, Burges	*Bashful Ballads*
Johnston, Alexander	*Ten and Out*
Joyce[?], P.W.	*Short Hist. of Gaelic Ireland*
Khayam	*The Rubyiat*
Kibbis[?], Henry	*Songs of the Trail*
Kipling, Rudyard	*The Jungle Book*
Kipling, Rudyard	*Lang and Sea Tales*
Kipling, Rudyard	*Kipling (1 vol)*
Kipling, Rudyard	*Phantom Rickshaw*
Kipling, Rudyard	*Kipling (verse inclusive ed.)*
Kubin, Alfred	*Damonem und Nachtgesichte*
Lamarre[?]	*The Rassi[?]n of the Beast*
Lanb, Harold	*The Crusades*
Larie & Poole	*Turkey*
Larson	*History of England*
Leonard	*Hundred Years of Missions*
Lincoln	*Cur. Making in Element. School (2 copies)*
Lippman	*Preface to Morals*
Little, W. Gordon	*Buffalo Bill*
Little Nature Library	*Garden Flowers*
Little Nature Library	*Trees*
Little Nature Library	*Wild Flowers*
Little Nature Library	*Birds Worth Knowing*
Little Nature Library	*Animals Worth Knowing*
Little Nature Library	*Butterflies*
London, Jack	*Faith of Men*
London, Jack	*The Human Drift*
London, Jack	*The Iron Heel*
London, Jack	*The Star P(r)ouer[?]*
London, Jack	*The Strenght of the Strong*
Lovecraft, H.P.	*Cats of Ulthar*
Lovecraft, H.P.	*The Shunned House*
Lucian	*The Mines of the Countesans*
Lyttle	*Bedfort F[?]Tronest[?]*
McGuffey	*Electric Speaker*
Maitland, Robert	*Boys Scouts to the Rescue*
Maitland, Robert	*The Boy Scouts in Camp*
Milton, John	*Works of Milton*
Mitchell, Cortes	*Montezuma and Mexico*

Mundy, Talbot	*The Eye of Zeitoon*
Mundy, Talbot	*Hira Singh* (2 copies)
Mundy, Talbot	*The Ivory Trail*
Mundy, Talbot	*King of the Khyben Rifles*
Mundy, Talbot	*Ring H___ the Ind ___* [??]
Mundy, Talbot	*The Winds of the World*
	Nature Almanac
Newcomb	*Astronomy for Everybody*
Nicolson, John U.	*The King of the Black Isles*
Northrop, Henry	*Marvels of Natural History*
Noyes, Alfred	*Tales of the Mermaid Tavern*

NOTE ON CONAN: PAPERBACK QUARTERLY, vol. 1
number 1, reported the presence of nine books
by Sir Arthur Conan Doyle in Robert E. Howard's
personal library. The article continued, "This
admiration for Sir Arthur Conan Doyle suggests a
source for the name of Howard's most popular
character--Conan." The comment elicited another
suggestion from Robert M. Williams. In a
letter printed in PQ #2, Mr. Williams suggested
that Howard may have been familiar with the
historical figure, Duke Conan IV, whose daughter
married the son of Henry II of England. Our
speculations about Howard's source for the name
"Conan" should include the simple dictionary
meaning. Conan is a Celtic name which indicates
masculinity and wisdom. Howard's interest in
Celtic mythology might have influenced him to
choose a Celtic name for his favorite character.

UNDERWOOD/MILLER RELEASE
NEW HOWARD EDITIONS

Most serious book collectors search not only
for a particular title but also for a particular
edition of a book. The binding, paper, illustrations...the physical quality of a book has a great
influence on its collectability. Indeed publishers themselves like Hogarth Press and Heritage
Press are collectable. One publisher which will
no doubt one day be collectable are the publishers
Tim Underwood and Chuck Miller. One book in
particular which stands out is their Always Comes
Evening, a 110 page book of poetry by Robert E.
Howard, compiled by Glenn Lord and illustrated by
Keiko Nelson. Always Comes Evening was originally
published by Arkhan House in 1957 with only a 636
copy edition. This long over due new edition is
artistically produced from cover to cover. Miller
and Underwood make use of an unique and very
appropiate print type as well as illustrations
which compliment Howard's poetry. They even make
successful use of the end papers. On the front
end paper a facsimile of one of REH's earliest
poems is reproduced in his own handwriting as well
as a type set reproduction. On the back end papers
is Frank Utpatel's drawing for the dust jacket
of the coveted original 1957 edition. Between
these end papers lies an unique and well planned
layout of Howard's verse. If your a Howard
collector, this book is a must. If your not,
then this book will make you want to be. Only $10.
A leatherbound limited edition(206 copies printed)
is available, signed by the artist for $31 with
slip case and additional handwritten facsimile of
Howard's "The Song of Yar Ali Kahn."
Another unique book in the Chuck Miller line
up is The Grey God Passes by Robert E. Howard.
The format of this publication is simular to PQ
though the quality is better by at least 10. Like
Always Comes Evening, the quality of the publicat-

ion matched with a quality writer makes this a good
buy. The superb illustrations by Walter Simonson
and the very readable print adds to this small
(36 pages) buy interesting Howard story of the
Viking wars. Only $4.
      Both books are available from Chuck Miller,
239 North 4th, Columbia, PA 17512.

THE 1978 WORLD FANTASY CONVENTION WILL BE HELD
IN FORT WORTH, TEXAS ON OCTOBER 13, 14, & 15.
MICHAEL TEMPLIN, 1309 S. WEST, ARLINGTON, TEXAS
76010 IS THE 1978 CHAIRMAN. THE CONVENTION WILL
HONOR THE LATE ROBERT E. HOWARD. MAKE PLANS TO
ATTEND!!

PAPERBACKS ON REVIEW

Spiderweb
by Robert Bloch
(Ace, 1954; D-59) 157 pp. 35¢

This is the story of a loser, Eddie haines,
who makes a bargain with the devil, in the person
of the mysterious Professor Hermann. You know
what happens to people who make bargains like that.
Eddie changes his name and his personality and
becomes a part of the professor's schemes, only
to discover that he wants out when it's too late.
The professor has already framed him for murder
and enmeshed him in a spiderweb of crime.

Actually, the professor is a con man in the
old California self-help tradition, and his
operation, YOU (Your Opportunities, Unlimited)
sounds a lot like est, or How To Be Your Own Best
Friend, or maybe Dianetics; but the professor's
purposes are sinister. He's out for his own gain,
no matter what happens to anyone else. When
Eddie tries to break away, he finds himself in
big trouble.

No one should read this book looking for
another Psycho, though there is one good, grisly
scene. It's simply a straightforward tale of a
man who gets in over his head and who tries to
get out, with the emphasis on action most of the
way. In addition, there are a number of interesting insights into how an organization such
as the professor's might actually work its
"miracles," and these insights are what keep the
book from seeming too old fashioned.

--------Bill Crider

Hordes of the Red Butcher
by Grant Stockbridge
(Pocket Books, 1975) 158 pp. 95¢

The cover states Spider Series #2, and
proudly proclaims "Spider sales over 20,000,000".
For those of you shose memories don't go that
far back, The Spider was one of the more popular
pulp heroes back in the '30s and '40s, with his
magazine running for 118 issues. But a casual
observer would never guess that by looking at
the cover. Pocket Books evidently decided to
pass The Spider off as some modern hero, abandon-
ing the nostalgic approach which brought so much
success to Doc Savage, The Avenger, and The
Shadow, to name a few.

Oh, this is one of the original novels, all
right. Copyright 1935, in fact. The problem is
that the original novel wasn't much in the first
place, and it wasn't helped by Pocket's vain
attempt to update it.

The novel opens with Richard Wenworth, Spider's
alter ego (the 'The' has been dropped, for some
odd reason) being a passenger on a train that is
ambushed in Kentucky by a horde of Neanderthals.
After brutally killing everyone on the train,
except for Spider, they depart. Except these are
evidently no ordinary Neanderthals, since they
seem to be practically impervious to bullets
(the only sure way to kill one being holding
a high powered pistol at the base of the skull,
firing at least five times, and run). But anyway, the novel drags on, the Neanderthals killing
and burning, and Spider searching for their leader,
the Headsman, rather ineptly. Once the Headsman
even got Spider sentenced to the electric chair!
Of course our hero escapes and captures the
Headsman while saving a town at the last possible
second from the cavemen. Finis.

All in all, it is a terrible book. Parts
of it are so gory that it makes Nick Carter,

Killmaster, look like someone out of Mother Goose.
No logical basis is given for the almost super-
human powers of the Neanderthals. And, the
attempt to set it in the '70s is a complete
failure. If I were Steve Lewis, I would give
this book an F.

--------Scott Owen
Moraga, California

The Alcoholics
by Jim Thompson
(Lion Books, 1953) 127 pp. 25¢

Jim Thompson was one of the best of the
paperback writers in the 1950's. Lion Books
(I suppose in all seriousness) nominated his
The Killer Inside Me for the National Book
Award, and R.V. Cassil titled his study of that
same book "Fear, Purgation, and Sophoclean Light."
(This essay appears in David Madden's Tough Guy
Writers of the Thirties.) Unfortunately, The
Alcoholics is not quite as good as The Killer....,
though it has its moments. It is supposed to be
the story of one day in a sanitarium, and it
does indeed present some powerful arguments
against alcoholism. Thompson writes realistically
and unsentimentally for the most part, but the
ending, with the sudden reformation of five
alcoholics, is far too pat. And the cure of the
sadistic nurse is not to be believed.
No book by Thompson is a total loss, however.
He has the power to shock and the ability to make
you care about his characters. His knowledge of
psychology is put to interesting use, too, as it
is in his best books, if not quite as convincingly.
While it might not make anyone a new fan of
Thompson's work, the book will be sought by all
Thompson collectors.

-------Bill Crider

Hanging Woman Creek
by Louis L'Amour
(Bantam 1964, 1971) 151 pp. 95¢

Mojave Crossing
by Louis L'Amour
(Bantam 1964, 1971) 148 pp. 75¢

Watching the 60 Minutes segment on Louis
L'Amour (August 13, 1978), I began to wonder
what I had been missing. After all, a writer
who has sold over 70 million books must have
something going. So I went out and picked up
two books at random and read them. I wish I
could remember exactly what it was that George
C. Scott said about western movies in They Might
Be Giants, because I believe he describes L'Amour's
books pretty well. I'll just have to paraphrase,
and add my own thoughts: There aren't any masses
in these two books, just individuals who make
their own choices; and those choices determine
the fates of the men who make them. The narrators
in these novels (Tell Sackett in Mojave Crossing,
Pronto Pike in Hanging Woman Creek) are strong
men, competent with their fists or with a gun.
They aren't handsome, but women admire them.
They are honest, and they have a code of honor
to which they will not be false, even if adhering
to the code may be dangerous. They do what they
have to do, go where they have to go. Evil in
the books is pretty clear cut--there's no doubting
who the bad guys are. L'Amour puts his characters,
good and bad, into fast-moving stories set very
firmly in the historical West. He seems, in fact,
a stickler for historical accuracy. Add to all
this the author's solid story-telling ability
and you have kind of popular fiction that may
well outlast some of today's prestigious writers
or "mainstream" works.

----------Bill Crider

11. The introduction of Pocket Books, Inc. by Robert de Graff in 1939 is considered by most to be the beginning of paperback publishing as we now know it. In that same year, Columbia Art Works, Inc. introduced a new paperback series under the name of Red Arrow Books. Columbia Art Works, Inc. at that time was a 35 year old printing, publishing, and lithographing company. According to Red Arrow Book number 3, <u>Murders in Praed Street</u>, Red Arrow Books...

RED ARROW BOOKS

Are composed in Baskerville type which is noted for its legibility. Ease of reading is further promoted by the width of line—"A-Line-at-a-Glance." Red Arrow Books are the first to be produced in Offset Lithography — which contributes unusual softness and excellence of printing. Light weight — averaging but six ounces — and modern wide-opening bindings afford additional comfort in reading.

Lastly, Red Arrow Books are easy to select: red covers denote Mystery and Crime stories — green covers denote Travel and Adventure — blue covers denote Fiction.

Only 12 titles were issued, all reprints, and sold for 25¢ each. Each book measured 4 & 3/8" by 7 & 1/16" in size. Their distribution was directed toward the magazine market rather than the book market. Though their Baskerville

print may have been high quality, their paper
was not. Unlike the high quality paper of early
Pocket Books, Red Arrow paper contains high acid
content resulting in yellowed and brittle paper.

The color of the covers designated the type
of book it was: a red cover was mystery & crime,
a green cover was travel and adventure, and a
blue cover was fiction. The back cover of Red
Arrow Book #3, Murders in Praed Street by John
Rhode lists all 12 books issued (see reproduction
in this issue). In a recent letter, M.C. Hill
of Bunker Books, P.O. BOX 1638, Spring Valley,
California who specializes in paperbacks from
1939-1959 states that he has Red Arrow Book #5,
but instead of a red cover, it has a black front
cover with green and white lettering and logo,
and a emerald green back cover. His Red Arrow
Book #4 has a blue-black front cover and a light
blue back cover. Both his books have 4 white
verticle 1/8th inch stripes on their left side.
Does anyone else have any additional information
on Red Arrow Books? Are there any more cover
color discrepancies?

--------Bill Simms
Washington DC

12. I am trying in vain to determine the
identity of the artists who drew the maps for
the early Dell paperbacks. I'm sure the artists
were at Western Printing, but I can't get any
further information. Not even Helen Meyer
(past President of Dell) or the Dell librarian
knows. Can anyone help? I am working on a book
dealing with all Dell books, 1942 to 1962, and
this information is essential.

-------Bill Lyles
Silver Spring, MD

RED ARROW BOOKS

MYSTERY & CRIME—Red Covers

1. THIRTEEN AT DINNER — Agatha Christie
2. MURDER ON HUDSON — Jennifer Jones
3. MURDERS IN PRAED STREET — John Rhode
4. DEATH IN THE LIBRARY — Philip Ketchum
5. DEATH WEARS A WHITE GARDENIA — Zelda Popkin

TRAVEL & ADVENTURE—Green Covers

6. MY SOUTH SEA ISLAND — Eric Musprat
7. YANKEE KOMISAR — Commander S. M.
8. GIRL HUNT — Laurence D. Smith
9. THE SEVEN SLEEPERS — Francis Beeding
10. CAPTAIN NEMESIS — F. Van Wyck Mason

FICTION—Blue Covers

11. WINDSWEPT — Olga Moore
12. PIRATE'S PURCHASE — Ben Ames Williams

NEW TITLES ADDED REGULARLY

RED ARROW BOOKS
1024-36 W. Juneau Ave.
Milwaukee, Wisconsin

13. From all indications, Dell 10¢ paperbacks
are hard to come by...their on everyone's want
list but not on anyone's selling list. For those
of you who have not seen very many 10¢ers, like
myself, the 1950 Publishers' Weekly might be of
interest. Page 525 of Vol. 159 contains 4 re-
productions of the 10¢ers with a short "first
announcement" note attached. Though the repro-
ductions are not very clear, they are worth
searching for.

------John Evans
New York, New York

14. I own perhaps one of the shortest (only 8
pages long) and one of the smallest (2 & 5/16"
by 2 & 14/16") murder mystery paperbacks every
printed. Its distributor, you might say, was
Big Thrill Chewing Gum and is copyrighted by
Whitman Publishing Co. in 1934. As denoted on
the back "cover", it is story number 2 of a
series of 30 thrilling Buck Jones Adventures.
Other series include Dick Tracy, Tailspin Tommy,
and Buck Rogers. Does anyone have any additional
information on these chewing gum "paperbacks"?

"We've got the goods on you, Gregg!" snapped Buck with a quick jerk at the rogue's shirt — and there, before the eyes of the gathered throng, was revealed a roll of crisp, new bills, drawn from the bank that day by Rusty's father.

"If you hadn't been so anxious to get rid of me," said Buck, "you might have got away with it!"

This is story No. 2 of a series of 30 thrilling BUCK JONES ADVENTURES. *Begin collecting the entire series today. Also other series of thrilling adventure stories featuring Dick Tracy—Tailspin Tommy—Buck Rogers.*

BIG THRILL
CHEWING GUM
THE GOUDEY GUM CO., BOSTON
Ⓓ1934   PRINTED IN U. S. A.

8

PAPER BACKS
1939-1959

THE FOLLOWING PAPERBACKS ARE
ALL GOOD MIXTURES OF SCIENCE
FICTION, MYSTERY, WESTERN, AD-
VENTURE, ROMANCE, ETC. AND WILL
GRADE FROM FAIR TO FINE. ALL
ARE FROM 1939-1959 AND ARE
WORTH DOUBLE THE PRICE ASKED
OR MORE. THEY ARE GOOD DEALER
OR COLLECTOR READING AND TRAD-
ING STOCK. EACH 10 ARE PLUS 64¢
POSTAGE. I PROVIDE THE INSUR
ANCE. BOOKS ARE MAILED OUT THE
SAME DAY ORDER IS RECEIVED.

10 DIFFERENT ACE D & S...$5.00

10 DIFFERENT DELL 25¢
   KEYHOLE-MAPBACKS......$6.00

10 DIFFERENT POCKET BOOKS$4.50

10 DIFFERENT MIXED AVON, LION,
   BANTAM, GRAFIC, GOLD MEDAL,
   SIGNET, PENGUIN,ETC...$4.00

BUNKER BOOKS
P.O. BOX 1638
SPRING VALLEY, CA. 92077

(714) 469-3296   WSA 418

HOWARD PAYNE UNIVERSITY

BROWNWOOD, TEXAS

PRESENTS

A COLLOQUIUM ON PAPERBACK BOOKS

FEBRUARY 22-24, 1979

A number of special sessions will be devoted to
papers on various aspects of paperback books.
Anyone wishing to contribute is asked to sent
a one-page resume of his paper by December 5, 1978.
(Final versions of all papers must be limited to
10 pages.) Some suggested topics:

1. Publishing histories of obscure paperback
    houses(Lion, Bart House,etc.) or major houses
    (Dell, Fawcett, Bantam,etc.)
2. Trends in paperback cover art (or discussion
    of specific artists)
3. Analyses of paperback writers whose work has
    been generally neglected by critics (Jim
    Thompson, Charles Williams, R.V. Cassil, etc.)
4. Series books (The Destroyer, The Executioner,
    Travis McGee, Matt Helm, etc.)
5. Publishing trends in original fiction
    ("backwoods" books, "sweet/savage" books,
    westerns, mysteries, etc.)

The above topics are merely suggestions. All
papers related directly to paperback books,
their authors, illustrators, publishers, or
distributors will be considered. The papers may
be approached from the point of view of popular
culture, bibliography, history, or literary
criticism. All papers read at the Colloquium will
also be considered for future publication in
PAPERBACK QUARTERLY.
Send all submissions to Bill Crider, Department
of English, Howard Payne University, Brownwood,
Texas 76801.

WILLIAM & PATRICIA LYLES
13810 CASTLE BLVD., APT. 304
SILVER SPRING, MD 20904
(301) 890-6412

WANTED:

DELL PAPERBACKS: 38,77,89,205,278,993
(all but the last joke & puzzle
books); 10¢ books 11,29,33; D162,
D236,D395,D427,F142,F156,F179,F186,
R119,X1.B134,B149,B161,B199,LC112,
LC129,LS102,Ls106,Visual Book VY4

FIRST EDITIONS BY CLAYTON RAWSON
PRE-1962 ISSUES OF PAPERBOUND BOOKS IN
    PRINT
ANYTHING BY JOLAN FOLDES(aka YOLANDA
    FOLDES)except GOLDEN ERRINGS and
    STREET OF THE FISHING CAT
FIRST EDITION OF ERROL FLYNN'S BEAM ENDS
DELL DIGEST-SIZED BOOKS, PARTICULARLY
    ZANE GREY'S WESTERN MAGAZINE
DELL MAGAZINE 1000 JOKES
DELL COMICS WITH MAPS ON COVERS
PAPERBACKS OTHER THAN DELL WITH MAPS ON
    BACK COVERS OR KEYHOLES ON FRONT
    COVERS
ANY DELL PAPERBACK WITH DUST JACKET
BOOKS BY JAMES THURBER AND OGDEN NASH
BOOKS ABOUT UNICORNS, WELL WRITTEN CAT
    MYSTERIES(NO LOCKRIDGES, PLEASE)
EDMUND CRISPIN'S DEAD AND DUMB and
    HOLY DISORDERS
AUTHOR BIBLIOGRAPHIES AT REASONABLE PRICES
STUDIES OF LESSER-KNOWN WRITERS

WE WOULD LIKE TO HEAR FROM ANYONE WHO HAS
USED THE CRIME MAPS WHILE READING THE DELL
EDITIONS---COMMENTS AS TO USEFULNESS,
ACCURACY, etc.

LORE-X

Published Quarterly

by

Martin E. Gottschalk
P. O. Box 851
Brownwood, Texas 76801

Editor

Bill Crider, Ph.D., Howard Payne University, Brownwood

Associate Editors

Lewis H. Miller, D.D., LL.D., 910 8th, Brownwood
Charlotte Laughlin, Ph.D., Howard Payne University, Brownwood
Elva Dobson, Poet, 2103 11th, Brownwood

Subscription Rates

Annual $5.00; Single copies $1.75

Correspondence and subscriptions should be sent to the publisher. Contributions of prose, verse and artwork will be considered which reflect the American culture. Manuscripts must be typewritten, up to twentyfive hundred words, double spaced and original, although any reasonable length will be considered. They should be addressed to the editor with the above address.

The purpose of this journal is to provide a medium for individuals who are devoted to the arts and humanities so that they may have an opportunity to express themselves and share with others.

S.H. OWEN

P.O. BOX 343

MORAGA, CALIFORNIA

94556

FOR SALE

DELLS	BANTAM
POPULAR LIBRARY	LION
POCKET BOOKS	GOLD MEDAL
SIGNET	AVON

AND MANY OTHERS

LOW PRICES!

LOTS AND LOTS OF BARGAINS

LIST 15¢

WANTED: (WILL TRADE OR BUY)

DELL 10¢	BART HOUSE
BANTAM LOS ANGELES	GRAPHIC

AND OTHERS

PLEASE QUOTE

BILL CRIDER
4206 Ninth Street
Brownwood, Texas 76801

WILL BUY OR TRADE

ACE DOUBLES: D-3,13,15,16,25,26,27,35,36,123,129,
     149,170,189,197,203,209,259,285,305,379,477.

ACE SINGLES: S-143,153,159;D-444.

By Jim Thompson:
BAD BOY
THE GRIFTERS
ROUGHNECK
SAVAGE NIGHT

By Charles Williams:
THE BIG BITE(Dell 1st only)
HILL GIRL(GM 1st only)

By Dan J. Marlowe:
THE FATAL FRAILS(Avon)

By Harry Whittington:
VENGEANCE VALLEY(Phoenix HC)
HER SIN(Phoenix HC)
THE LADY WAS A TRAMP(Handi)
FOREVER EVIL
SWAMP KILL
SATAN'S WIDOW(Phantom)
CRACKER GIRL(Beacon)
WILD OATS(Beacon)
PRIME SUCKER(Beacon)
A WOMAN ON THE PLACE(Ace)
MINK
STAR LUST(Avon)
THE DEVIL WEARS WINGS
REBEL WOMAN(Avon)
STRICTLY FOR THE BOYS(Stanley)
TREACHERY TRAIL
THE SMELL OF JASMINE(Avon)

By Clay Stuart:
HIS BROTHER'S WIFE
    (Beacon)

By Hallam Whitney:
SHACK ROAD
CITY GIRL
BACKWOODS SHACK
WILD SEED(Ace)

By Whit Harrison:
BODY AND PASSION
GIRL ON PAROLE
SHANTY ROAD
STRIP THE TOWN NAKED
    (Beacon)
ANY WOMAN HE WANTED
    (Beacon)
A WOMAN POSSESSED
    (Beacon)
VIOLENT NIGHT(Phantom)
SWAMP KILL(Phantom)

By Henry Kuttner:
MURDER OF A WIFE(PERMA)

By Kell Holland
THE TEMPTED(Beacon)

By Jada Davis:
ONE FOR HELL(Red Seal)

63

```
*************************************************
*                                               *
*          COMING IN THE NEXT ISSUE             *
*          OF PAPERBACK QUARTERLY               *
*                                               *
*                                               *
*     PAUL HAMMONDS'S COLUMN " INDEX OF         *
*          PUBLISHERS' WEEKLY"                  *
*                                               *
*     BILL CRIDER'S COLUMN "PAPERBACK           *
*          WRITERS"                             *
*                                               *
*     GEORGE KELLEY'S COLUMN "TEN BOOKS"        *
*                                               *
*     CONTINUATION OF THE CHECK LIST OF         *
*     ROBERT E. HOWARD'S LIBRARY                *
*                                               *
*     PQ INTERVIEW WITH AUTHOR BRUNO            *
*          FISCHER                              *
*                                               *
```

Bruno Fischer

```
*     MORE ARTICLES                             *
*                                               *
*     MORE REVIEWS                              *
*                                               *
*     MORE NOTES AND QUERIES                    *
*                                               *
*************************************************
```

www.ingramcontent.com/pod-product-compliance
Lightning Source LLC
Chambersburg PA
CBHW011439170626
46808CB00009B/3108